YOUR KNOWLEDGE HAS VALUE

AF301376

- We will publish your bachelor's and
  master's thesis, essays and papers

- Your own eBook and book -
  sold worldwide in all relevant shops

- Earn money with each sale

Upload your text at www.GRIN.com
and publish for free

Bibliographic information published by the German National Library:

The German National Library lists this publication in the National Bibliography;
detailed bibliographic data are available on the Internet at http://dnb.dnb.de .

Imprint:

Copyright © 2005 GRIN Verlag, Open Publishing GmbH
Print and binding: Books on Demand GmbH, Norderstedt Germany
ISBN: 9783668085619

This book at GRIN:

http://www.grin.com/en/e-book/145502/john-lewis-partnership-s-leadership-a-case-study

Miriam Mennen

John Lewis Partnership's leadership. A case study

GRIN Publishing

In this essay John Lewis Partnership's leadership is going to be examined. First, company's main events will be highlighted. Furthermore, theories of leadership and mostly democratic will be analysed and then will be applied to the company's profile.

The company's interesting history begins in 1864, when John Lewis opened his first shop on Oxford Street, London. Nowadays, the partnership hires over 63,000 employees – partners and consists of 27 John Lewis department stores and 166 Waitrose supermarkets. The most important facts which are highlighted in the Partnership's history are the above:

i)   The publication of the first constitution, 1928.

ii)   The creation of the first Trust Settlement - The John Lewis Partnership becomes legal. All the profits are available for distribution amongst the Partners, 1929.

iii)   The second Trust Settlement – Provides for the election of some directors and the appointment of the chairman – All members should have the ability of sharing the advantages of ownership, 1950.

John Lewis had a vision which was clearly reflected by the words of his son Spedan Lewis, who reformed a simple company to a prototype which centres the interest of anyone's who comes across with this company. The company's purpose is highlighted in the partnership's constitution 'The Partnership's ultimate purpose is the happiness of all its members, through their worthwhile and satisfying employment in a successful business. Because the Partnership is owned in trust for its members, they share the responsibilities of ownership as well as its rewards – profit, knowledge and power'. How power is shared? It is generally described on the constitution's first rule: 'The Partnership operates on democratic principles and as much sharing of power among its members as is consistent with efficiency'.

There are many opinions on how a good leader is being made. One viewpoint is held by Professor John Hunt, professor of Organisational Behaviour at London Business School, who has conducted research into leadership for several years.

To quote Harold Leavitt (1969): "Authority does not make men leaders. Skill in using authority or personal attributes to build a problem solving organisation probably does help make men leaders". This gives us a helpful introduction into the concept of leadership. There are those that are naturally leaders and others will always follow them. In the work place, the responsibility is normally on management or supervisors to provide the leading role. There are a number of styles evident in the way this role is carried out, and this has a direct effect on how employees will perform.

Cole (1986) set out a good description of the types of leadership and the theories of leadership, which are briefly outlined below. Cole identifies five main types of leadership:

i) The <u>Charismatic</u> leader - the basis of this is personality and there are not many whose personality can turn all those around them into followers. Examples of this type of leader are Napoleon, Hitler, Churchill

ii) The <u>Traditional</u> leader - someone "whose position is assured by birth" (Cole 1986), for example kings, queens, tribal chieftains.

iii) The <u>Situational</u> leader - "whose influence can only be effective by being in the right place at the right time" (Cole 1986)

iv) The <u>Appointed</u> leader - "whose influence arises directly out of his position" (Cole, 1986) For example most managers and supervisors.

v) The <u>Functional</u> leader - "who secures his leadership position by what he does, rather than by what he is" (Cole, 1986). This is someone who adapts behaviour to meet the requirements of the situation.

Cole goes on to say that leadership "is intimately linked to behaviour" and "can be described as a dynamic process in a group whereby one individual influences the others to contribute voluntarily to the achievement of group tasks in a given situation". This is an issue of relevance to the project and will contribute towards the later study.

As leadership is a dynamic process, it is that there is a range of styles to fit in with different individuals, groups and situations, rather than one style. As Cole points out " the role of the leader is to direct the group towards group goals. The style of the leadership and the reaction of the group will be determined considerably by the situation concerned (the task, external pressures, etc.)" (1986).

This leads us to examine the leadership variables, which are the skills, knowledge and personality of the leader, the tasks or goals that must be achieved, the skills and motivation of the group members or subordinates and finally the environment or situation they find themselves in. As Cole states " taken together these variables form the total leadership situation...the art of leadership is to find the best balance between them in the light of the whole situation" (1986).

Cole then examines the various theories of leadership, of which there are three main categories:

i) The **Trait** Theories, which are based on the personal characteristics of the leader

ii) The **Style** Theories, which are based on leader behaviour

iii) The **Contingency** Theories, which are based on leader behaviour adapting according to the situation.

With regard to workplace structure, Buchanan and Huczynski, point out that "there is evidence to suggest that group performance and satisfaction is affected by the type of leadership exercised within a group" (1997). They go on to describe a study undertaken in the 1950's by White and Lippitt, who looked at the effects that different styles of leadership had on the behaviour of groups, in their case a group of youths. Their research involved three styles of leadership:

i)"democratic" (where "policies were determined by group discussion and decision" and "the leader encouraged and assisted the group in this process"),

ii)"authoritarian" (where "all the policies of the group were determined solely by the leader") and

iii)"laissez faire" (where "there was a minimum of leader participation and members (of the group) were left to make their own individual or group decisions").

Leadership treatments

Authoritarian	Democratic	Laissez-faire
1: All determination of policy by the leader	1: All policies a matter of group discussion and decision, encouraged and assisted by the leader	1: Complete freedom for group or individual decision, with a minimum of leader participation
2: Techniques and activity steps dictated by the authority, one at a time, so the future steps were always uncertain to a large degree	2: Activity perspective gained during discussion period. General steps to group goal sketched and when technical advice was needed, the leader suggested two or more alternative procedures from which choice could be made.	2: Various materials supplied by the leader, who made it clear that he would supply information when asked. He took no other part in work discussion
3: The leader usually dictated the particular work task and work companion of each member	3: The members were free to work with whomever they chose, and the division of tasks was left up to the group	3: Complete non-participation of the leader
4: The dominator tended to be 'personal' in his praise and criticism of the work of each member; remained aloof from active group participation except when demonstrating	4: The leader was 'objective' or 'fact-minded' in his praise and criticism, and tried to be a regular group member in spirit without doing too much of the work	4: Infrequent spontaneous comments on member activities unless questioned, and no attempt to appraise or regulate the course of events

(Source: Buchanan & Huczynski, 1997)

After careful study it was found the "each of the different leadership styles evoked different behaviour among the group members". The effects were found to be as follows:

Having <u>democratic leadership</u>, the relations between members were friendlier. Whilst, more individual differences were shown, there 'was also a high degree of group-mindedness'. Overall the group produced better results.

<u>In laissez-faire leadership</u>, the group seemed to lack direction but is the ability to make group decisions and overall achievement.

In the <u>authoritarian leadership</u>, the observations showed two types of reaction, "one was aggressive while the other was apathetic".

The biggest differences were observed among two types of leadership , authoritarian and democratic. In the diagram below we can criticize the main differences between authoritarian and democratic leadership.

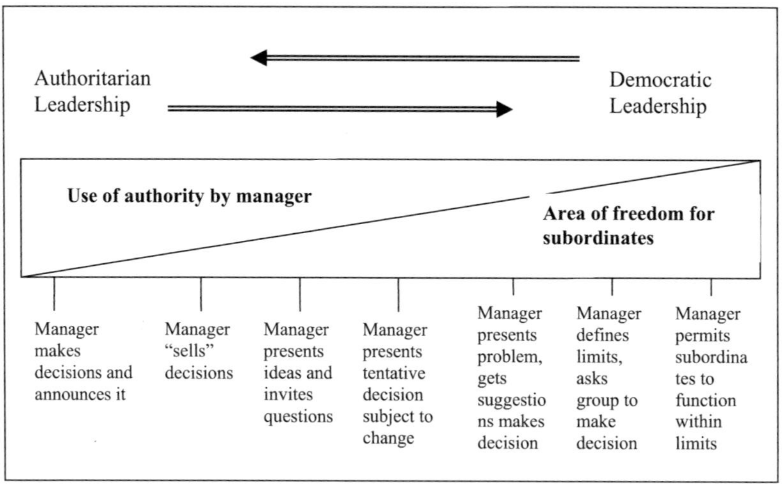

(Adopted from Daft, R (1999) p. 71)

Is it risky having a sole leader running a company or having a vast number of people - partners making decisions upon the company's future? Leadership can be taken more like a form of art than of science. It is not only the theory that counts but the ability of handling opportunities and coordinating people having the same vision.

The partnership's philosophy can be reflected from a statement which was made by the company's chairman Sir Stuart Hampson on the Independent: 'The fundamentals of our business, the principles we were founded upon, are still very relevant today.'

Democracy established in a company… Is that possible nowadays when most of times the main purpose of business are profit and just profit? Especially in England, a country which is definitely capitalistic, it is quite remarkable finding this type of business structure.

Democratic procedures are followed on every aspect. In the diagrams below we can observe the company's decision making structure:

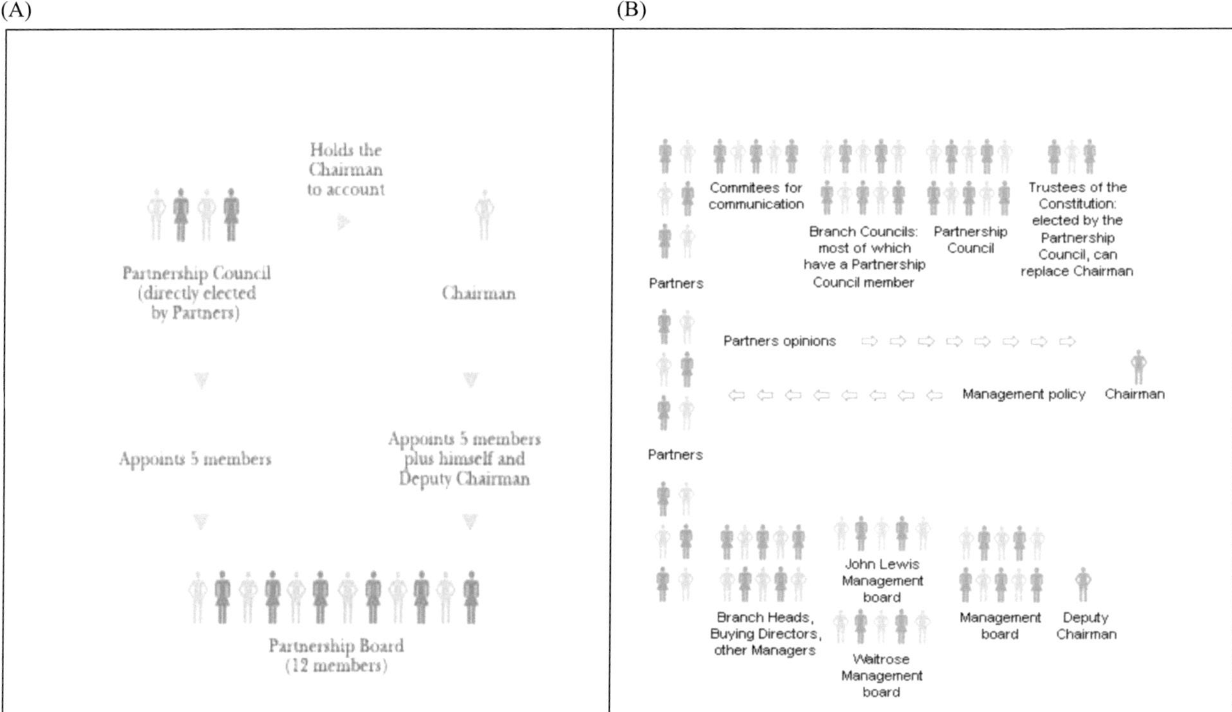

(Source: http://www.johnlewispartnership.co.uk/)

At first sight, the diagrams may seem complex and unusual when the only matter is profit and normally the decisions should be made by those who have position and money power. John Lewis's democratic leadership can be explained as follows:

In diagram (A) we can see that John Lewis has three effective authorities: the Chairman; the Partnership Council and the Central Board. Central board consists of 12 directors: the chairman and deputy chairman, five directors appointed by the chairman and five elected by the Partnership Council. The chairman may have great power, but if he does not exercise it in an acceptable manner, always in accordance with the constitution, the members of the Partnership Council can remove him from his position. Apart from the above, Partnership Council has other everyday activities. It is responsible for the internal communication with the administration and informing of the employees – partners about the company's activities. This can be achieved by publishing Staff Journals like The Gazette and the Chronicle and preserving an Internet Page, Partner Connect, where all partners can post their opinion about the company. In order to succeed in these democratic procedures all mechanisms and all members should cooperate in harmony.

Currently, Partnership council has approximately 130 members. The chairman appoints some members, usually from senior management, no more than one-fifth of the membership. The other members are being elected yearly anonymously by each employee – partner in the company. I can definitely talk about democracy in this company because the articles and rules of the constitution cannot be altered without its agreement. The council has its own income, guaranteed by the constitution in order to help partners and pensioners who are facing financial difficulties and for charities. The chairman as I wrote before cannot act on his/her own. If the chairman wants to reject a Partnership Council's decision he/she will first have to advise the Partnership Board.

For what it counts, every employee-partner has the ability to participate in the company's administration. Even though, his/her ambitions are not too high. At this point I can see a clear separation between ambition for position promotion and participation in leadership.

As a result of the above, freedom of word and act created strong bonds between the company's partners. A sense of belonging, being part of a united family was sensed as all of the employees enjoyed benefits like: pension, medical care, maternity and paternity pay, many social, leisure events and holiday centres.

Every partner can share an equal percentage of the company's profit, annually. Though, it's kind of ironic because all of the partners are not equally paid.

John Lewis also has a registry system. The Registrars are working alongside the heads of most branches. Their main role, apart from keeping personnel records, is to see that management, other partners and the representative institutions operate within the firm's constitution.

In diagram (B) we can see the partnership's communication model. Everyone from the least paid employee – partner has the right to express his/her opinion which, via company's forums, will directly be transferred to the partnership's decision making centres. But what is more interesting to me? They will have a direct answer. Well, in many other leadership models the heading officers would not bother to answer or give proper explanations to a low rank employee.

On the other hand, many problems have arisen when an internal survey was conducted by the partnership few months ago. The problems which were located were unfair payment and the administration processes, what an irony again, are not straightforward. Even democratic companies do have important issues to solve! In addition to other companies which probably do not even care to find out if their employees are happy when working or do have any suggestions to improve the company's internal functions.

What should really consider the managing boards are the administrative processes. Is it difficult to keep a leadership in such democratic levels and then expect from the employees to understand the company's functions completely, or are the employees right? A comment that can be made is that year by year the partnership is expanding; new stores and supermarkets are being opened.

Surely, the number of the 63,000 partners will be raised and trying to be so democratic will be getting more and more difficult.

Finally, in companies with democratic leadership you have many rights and benefits but many obligations as well. In antithesis to companies which have authoritarian leadership where you have less rights and benefits than obligations. In general, is everything about profit and money? Being pioneer and creating a democratic culture in business is somehow admirable!

References

Books:

- Buchanan, D. & Huczynski, A., (1997), *Organisational Behaviour*, 3rd edition, Prentice Hall
- Cole, G., (1986), *Management Theory and Practice*, DP Publications
- Daft, R., (1999), *Leadership: Theory and Practice*, The Dryden Press
- Leavitt, H., (1969), *Managerial Psychology*, University of Chicago Press

Journals and articles:

- Dandy, J. (1996). *The ethical route to service quality at John Lewis Partnership. Managing Service Quality.* 6 (5) , pp.17-19.
- Mesure, S. (2005). *The Interview: Urbane retailer who is never knowingly overstated.* [Internet] Available from: www.Independent.co.uk

Internet sources:

- www.Johnlewispartnership.co.uk

YOUR KNOWLEDGE HAS VALUE

- We will publish your bachelor's and
  master's thesis, essays and papers

- Your own eBook and book -
  sold worldwide in all relevant shops

- Earn money with each sale

Upload your text at www.GRIN.com
and publish for free